Breaking the CODE with Cryptography

Analyzing Patterns

Janey Levy

PowerMath™

The Rosen Publishing Group's

PowerKids Press™

New York

Published in 2007 by The Rosen Publishing Group, Inc.
29 East 21st Street, New York, NY 10010

Book Design: Daniel Hosek

Photo Credits: pp. 7, 11, 13 © Bettmann/Corbis; p. 9 © Corbis; pp. 17, 21 © Archivo Iconografico,
S.A./Corbis; p. 24 © Vanni Archive/Corbis; p. 29 © Fine Art Photographic Library/Corbis.

Library of Congress Cataloging-in-Publication Data

Levy, Janey.
  Breaking the code with cryptography : analyzing patterns / Janey Levy.
      p. cm. — (Math for the real world)
  Includes index.
  ISBN 1-4042-3368-7 (lib. bdg.)
  ISBN 1-4042-6089-7 (pbk.)
  6-pack ISBN 1-4042-6090-0
  1. Cryptography—Juvenile literature. 2. Ciphers—Juvenile literature. I. Title. II. Series.
  Z103.3.L47 2006
  652'.8—dc22
                                    2005014705

Manufactured in the United States of America

Contents

The year is 47 B.C. The location is Alexandria, Egypt. Julius Caesar, ruler of Rome and its territories, is fighting to conquer Egypt. After months of fighting, Caesar cannot defeat his enemy. Something has to be done. He prepares a message to send. He is careful to disguise the message so it can't be read if his enemies capture it. Caesar writes something like this:

LQ WURXEOH. QHHG PRUH VROGLHUV.

Soon more soldiers arrive. With their help, Caesar defeats the Egyptian army.

Caesar used **cryptography** in his message. He took his original message, called the plaintext, and used a **cipher** to **encrypt** it. The encrypted message, called the ciphertext, was the one he sent. The men who received the message knew the cipher Caesar used and used it to **decrypt** the message.

The need to send secret messages that can only be read by those they were meant for has existed for thousands of years. Over the centuries, many kinds of ciphers have been created. All ciphers depend on some kind of pattern. In this book, we're going to explore a few ciphers and learn how to find the pattern so we can decode the message. Keep reading to find out what Caesar's message said.

ITALY

Rome

Mediterranean Sea

Alexandria

EGYPT

Any message Caesar sent from Alexandria to Rome had to travel a great distance. Enemies would have had many opportunities to capture the messenger and the message. If Caesar's enemies could read his messages, they would learn valuable information that could help them defeat him. Secret messages were the only way to prevent that.

A Simple Substitution Cipher

Caesar used a simple substitution cipher. In a substitution cipher, each letter of the alphabet is replaced by another letter according to a rule or pattern. Caesar's cipher replaces each letter by the letter 3 places further along in the alphabet. In other words, it shifts each letter 3 letters to the right. *A* becomes *D, B* becomes *E,* and so on. You can think of this as creating a new alphabet that starts with the letter *D* instead of *A.* The new alphabet, called the ciphertext alphabet, is used to write the encrypted message. We can write the regular or plaintext alphabet above the ciphertext alphabet to see how the letters in the 2 alphabets correspond to each other. To encrypt a message, we would locate each letter of the message in the plaintext alphabet, then find the letter of the ciphertext alphabet that corresponds to it and substitute that letter. This is what Caesar did.

Plaintext alphabet: A B C D E F G H I J K L M N O P Q R S T U V W X Y Z
Ciphertext alphabet: D E F G H I J K L M N O P Q R S T U V W X Y Z A B C

Cryptography seems to have been invented about 4,500 years ago in ancient Egypt as a mental game to amuse the well-educated. Caesar, shown in this statue, is considered one of the first people to have used cryptography for the purpose of securing messages.

To decrypt Caesar's ciphertext, the men who received the message performed the operation in reverse. We can do the same. Here's Caesar's ciphertext again: LQ WURXEOH. QHHG PRUH VROGLHUV. Find each letter in the ciphertext in the ciphertext alphabet on the opposite page, then look at the plaintext alphabet above it to see what the letter should be.

LQ WURXEOH. QHHG PRUH VROGLHUV.
IN TROUBLE. NEED MORE SOLDIERS.

The kind of substitution cipher used by Caesar is called a shift cipher because it shifts each letter. Since Caesar is believed to have been the first to use a shift cipher, it is also known as a Caesar cipher. Caesar used a shift of 3 places to the right, but a shift or Caesar cipher may use a shift of any number of places. For example, we could create a Caesar cipher with a shift of 5 places to the right.

Plaintext alphabet: A B C D E F G H I J K L M N O P Q R S T U V W X Y Z
Ciphertext alphabet: F G H I J K L M N O P Q R S T U V W X Y Z A B C D E

Using this ciphertext alphabet, what would Caesar's message look like?

Suppose you've captured a **cryptogram** written in a shift or Caesar cipher. This is the message:

KV KU WTIGPV VJCV YG OGGV CV QPEG. QWT RNCPU JCXG DGGP FKUEQXGTGF. YG OWUV FGEKFG QP CPQVJGT RNCP.

You don't know what shift was used. How would you **cryptanalyze** the message? You would begin by trying to identify what plaintext letters some of the ciphertext letters stand for. Once you've done that, you'll be able to determine the pattern—that is, you'll be able to figure out what shift was used. That will enable you to decrypt the message.

According to the ancient Greek historian Herodotus, shown in this statue, the ancient Greeks had ways to send secret messages that did not use ciphers. They sometimes wrote a secret message on a wooden tablet, then covered it with wax. They were also known to tattoo a message on a slave's head. The slave's hair concealed the message.

How would you go about identifying what plaintext letters some of the ciphertext letters stand for in the cryptograms on page 8? One approach, known as frequency analysis, makes use of the fact that certain letters occur more frequently than others in the English language. The 3 most commonly occurring letters in English are *E, T,* and *N,* in that order. To see what letters of the ciphertext alphabet might stand for those letters, count how many times each letter appears in the encrypted message.

A	B	C	D	E	F	G	H	I	J	K	L	M	N	O	P	Q	R	S	T	U	V	W	X	Y	Z
0	0	6	1	3	4	14	0	1	3	4	0	0	2	2	7	5	2	0	4	4	8	3	2	2	0

G occurs far more often than any other letter in the encrypted message. *V* is next, then *P*. So perhaps *G = E, V = T,* and *P = N.* See what happens when you make these substitutions.

K	V		K	U		W	T	I		G	P	V		V	J	C	V		Y	G		O	G	G	V
	T									E	N	T		T			T			E			E	E	T

C	V		Q	P	E	G	.		Q	W	T		R	N	C	P	U		J	C	X	G
	T			N		E	.									N						E

D	G	G	P		F	K	U	E	Q	X	G	T	G	F	.		Y	G		O	W	U	V
	E	E	N					E			E		E		.			E					T

F	G	E	K	F	G		Q	P		C	P	Q	V	J	G	T		R	N	C	P	.
	E				E			N			N		T		E						N	.

10

This looks promising. There are no odd groupings of letters in the decryption that would suggest you're on the wrong track. The next step is to make use of the fact that certain 2-letter words appear more frequently in English than others. The most commonly occurring 2-letter words are *OF, TO, IN, IS, IT, BE, BY, HE, AS, ON, AT, OR, AN, SO, IF,* and *NO.* The following 2-letter words appear in the encrypted message: *KV, KU, YG, CV,* and *QP,* with *YG* appearing twice. Start with *KV,* since it is the first word in the message. You already have guessed the *V* may be *T. IT* and *AT* are both common 2-letter words in English, so perhaps *K* is *I* or *A.* The word *IT* would be a reasonable start for a sentence, so choose *K = I.*

Frequency analysis, the study of the frequency of letters, groups of letters, numbers, or symbols in a ciphertext, was invented by Arabs around A.D. 1000. This picture of an Arab man comes from a manuscript in the late 1400s.

Study the encrypted message again. You'll notice that 2 words in the message are almost identical: *RNCPU* and *RNCP*. Perhaps *RNCPU* is a plural form of *RNCP*. In that case, *U* would be *S*.

Now look at the guesses you've made so far: *G = E, V = T, P = N, K = I,* and *U = S*. A pattern emerges. Each ciphertext letter in this group is 2 letters to the right of the plaintext letter you think it might stand for. Write out the plaintext and ciphertext alphabets based on this pattern, use them to decrypt the message, and see if it makes sense.

Plaintext alphabet: A B C D E F G H I J K L M N O P Q R S T U V W X Y Z
Ciphertext alphabet: C D E F G H I J K L M N O P Q R S T U V W X Y Z A B

K	V		K	U		W	T	I		G	P	V		V	J	C	V		Y	G		O	G	G	V
I	T		I	S		U	R	G		E	N	T		T	H	A	T		W	E		M	E	E	T

C	V		Q	P	E	G	.		Q	W	T		R	N	C	P	U		J	C	X	G
A	T		O	N	C	E	.		O	U	R		P	L	A	N	S		H	A	V	E

D	G	G	P		F	K	U	E	Q	X	G	T	G	F	.		Y	G		O	W	U	V
B	E	E	N		D	I	S	C	O	V	E	R	E	D	.		W	E		M	U	S	T

F	G	E	K	F	G		Q	P		C	P	Q	V	J	G	T		R	N	C	P	.
D	E	C	I	D	E		O	N		A	N	O	T	H	E	R		P	L	A	N	.

In *The Adventures of the Dancing Men,* the famous fictional detective Sherlock Holmes explains a simple substitution cryptogram. This photograph shows the actor Basil Rathbone playing Sherlock Holmes in a movie.

The message makes perfect sense. The pattern you found is the correct one.

As you can see from your experience with this cryptogram, a Caesar cipher can be cryptanalyzed fairly quickly. This is not a desirable quality in an encryption system, so **cryptographers** developed methods to make Caesar ciphers harder to decrypt. We'll look at one of those next, along with some substitution ciphers that are not Caesar ciphers.

Other Simple Substitution Ciphers

In the cryptanalysis you just completed, each word in the ciphertext was the same length as the plaintext word it replaced. This made cryptanalyzing the message easier. As you made guesses about which ciphertext letters stood for which plaintext letters, you could look at the resulting patterns of letters to see if they were reasonable for English words. To aid in your cryptanalysis, you also made use of the fact that there were several 2-letter words in the cryptogram and that certain 2-letter words occur more frequently than others in English. You would not have been able to do these things if each word in the cryptogram had been of a fixed length in order to hide the lengths of the words in the plaintext message. For example, the length of each word in the ciphertext could be set at 5 letters. Using this system, Caesar's message from page 4 would look like this:

LQWUR XEOHQ HHGPR UHVRO GLHUV

Without the clues provided by the lengths of the words, it would be more difficult to cryptanalyze this message.

Can you read this message written with a Caesar cipher? Here is a clue: $H = E$.

VHFUH WPHVV DJHVV KRXOG VWDBV HFUHW

Answer: SECRET MESSAGES SHOULD STAY SECRET.

There are other substitution ciphers that are not Caesar ciphers. One famous substitution cipher, known as the Atbash cipher, was invented by **Hebrew** scholars around 550 B.C. It looks like this:

A	B	C	D	E	F	G	H	I	J	K	L	M
Z	Y	X	W	V	U	T	S	R	Q	P	O	N

Can you see the pattern in the Atbash cipher? The first half of the alphabet is paired with the last half in reverse order. When someone writes an encrypted message with the Atbash cipher, each letter becomes the one it is paired with. *A becomes Z, Z becomes A, B becomes Y, Y becomes B,* and so on. This is known as a **reciprocal** cipher. Can you read the message below written with the Atbash cipher?

HLNV KVLKOV VMQLB VMXIBKGRMT ZMW WVXIBKGRMT NVHHZTVH.

Answer: SOME PEOPLE ENJOY ENCRYPTING AND DECRYPTING MESSAGES.

A substitution cipher can also be made by replacing the letters of the alphabet with numbers and symbols. Frequency analysis can still be used to cryptanalyze this kind of substitution cipher. However, since the choices of numbers and symbols can be completely random, the cipher is harder to crack. Here is an example of a substitution cipher that uses numbers and symbols:

A	B	C	D	E	F	G	H	I	J	K	L	M	N	O	P	Q	R	S	T	U	V	W	X	Y	Z
!	@	#	$	%	^	&	*	+	=	<	>	?	~	(	:	)	1	2	3	4	5	6	7	8	9

Can you encrypt the message below using this cipher?

IMAGINE WHAT CAESAR WOULD THINK OF ALL THESE CIPHERS.

Answer: +?*&+~% 6*!3 #!%2!1 6(4>$ 3*+~< (^ !>> 3*%2% #+:*%12.

15

Polyalphabetic Substitution Ciphers

All simple substitution ciphers have a major weakness: they can be decrypted using frequency analysis. Cryptographers began trying to develop ciphers that could not be broken with this method. One solution they came up with was the **polyalphabetic** substitution cipher. A polyalphabetic substitution cipher uses more than 1 alphabet to encrypt a message. As a result, each letter in the plaintext message is encrypted by several different letters in the ciphertext, concealing the frequency with which it occurs.

One of the most famous polyalphabetic substitution ciphers was invented by the sixteenth-century French cryptographer Blaise de Vigenère (BLAYZ duh veej-NEHR). The Vigenère cipher is based on the following table:

	A	B	C	D	E	F	G	H	I	J	K	L	M	N	O	P	Q	R	S	T	U	V	W	X	Y	Z
A	A	B	C	D	E	F	G	H	I	J	K	L	M	N	O	P	Q	R	S	T	U	V	W	X	Y	Z
B	B	C	D	E	F	G	H	I	J	K	L	M	N	O	P	Q	R	S	T	U	V	W	X	Y	Z	A
C	C	D	E	F	G	H	I	J	K	L	M	N	O	P	Q	R	S	T	U	V	W	X	Y	Z	A	B
D	D	E	F	G	H	I	J	K	L	M	N	O	P	Q	R	S	T	U	V	W	X	Y	Z	A	B	C
E	E	F	G	H	I	J	K	L	M	N	O	P	Q	R	S	T	U	V	W	X	Y	Z	A	B	C	D
F	F	G	H	I	J	K	L	M	N	O	P	Q	R	S	T	U	V	W	X	Y	Z	A	B	C	D	E
G	G	H	I	J	K	L	M	N	O	P	Q	R	S	T	U	V	W	X	Y	Z	A	B	C	D	E	F
H	H	I	J	K	L	M	N	O	P	Q	R	S	T	U	V	W	X	Y	Z	A	B	C	D	E	F	G
I	I	J	K	L	M	N	O	P	Q	R	S	T	U	V	W	X	Y	Z	A	B	C	D	E	F	G	H
J	J	K	L	M	N	O	P	Q	R	S	T	U	V	W	X	Y	Z	A	B	C	D	E	F	G	H	I
K	K	L	M	N	O	P	Q	R	S	T	U	V	W	X	Y	Z	A	B	C	D	E	F	G	H	I	J
L	L	M	N	O	P	Q	R	S	T	U	V	W	X	Y	Z	A	B	C	D	E	F	G	H	I	J	K
M	M	N	O	P	Q	R	S	T	U	V	W	X	Y	Z	A	B	C	D	E	F	G	H	I	J	K	L
N	N	O	P	Q	R	S	T	U	V	W	X	Y	Z	A	B	C	D	E	F	G	H	I	J	K	L	M
O	O	P	Q	R	S	T	U	V	W	X	Y	Z	A	B	C	D	E	F	G	H	I	J	K	L	M	N
P	P	Q	R	S	T	U	V	W	X	Y	Z	A	B	C	D	E	F	G	H	I	J	K	L	M	N	O
Q	Q	R	S	T	U	V	W	X	Y	Z	A	B	C	D	E	F	G	H	I	J	K	L	M	N	O	P
R	R	S	T	U	V	W	X	Y	Z	A	B	C	D	E	F	G	H	I	J	K	L	M	N	O	P	Q
S	S	T	U	V	W	X	Y	Z	A	B	C	D	E	F	G	H	I	J	K	L	M	N	O	P	Q	R
T	T	U	V	W	X	Y	Z	A	B	C	D	E	F	G	H	I	J	K	L	M	N	O	P	Q	R	S
U	U	V	W	X	Y	Z	A	B	C	D	E	F	G	H	I	J	K	L	M	N	O	P	Q	R	S	T
V	V	W	X	Y	Z	A	B	C	D	E	F	G	H	I	J	K	L	M	N	O	P	Q	R	S	T	U
W	W	X	Y	Z	A	B	C	D	E	F	G	H	I	J	K	L	M	N	O	P	Q	R	S	T	U	V
X	X	Y	Z	A	B	C	D	E	F	G	H	I	J	K	L	M	N	O	P	Q	R	S	T	U	V	W
Y	Y	Z	A	B	C	D	E	F	G	H	I	J	K	L	M	N	O	P	Q	R	S	T	U	V	W	X
Z	Z	A	B	C	D	E	F	G	H	I	J	K	L	M	N	O	P	Q	R	S	T	U	V	W	X	Y

Notice that the alphabet in each row of the table is actually a Caesar cipher. The first row has a shift of 0, which means that it matches the plaintext alphabet. The second row has a shift of 1, the third row has a shift of 2, and so on.

The Vigenère cipher uses this table and a **keyword** to encrypt a message. Let's go through the process step-by-step using the following message as an example:

THE VIGENERE CIPHER MAKES CRYPTANALYSIS MORE CHALLENGING.

We'll start by rewriting the message in 5-letter words to conceal the lengths of the original words:

THEVI GENER ECIPH ERMAK ESCRY PTANA LYSIS MOREC HALLE NGING.

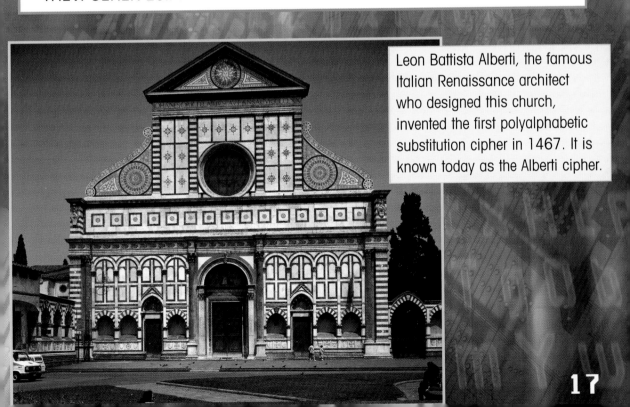

Leon Battista Alberti, the famous Italian Renaissance architect who designed this church, invented the first polyalphabetic substitution cipher in 1467. It is known today as the Alberti cipher.

Next, we'll choose a keyword. The keyword can be any word we want. Let's choose *ALBERTI*. We'll write the keyword above the plaintext, repeating it as many times as necessary.

Keyword: ALBER TIALB ERTIA LBERT IALBE RTIAL BERTI ALBER TIALB ERTIA
Plaintext: THEVI GENER ECIPH ERMAK ESCRY PTANA LYSIS MOREC HALLE NGING

Now we'll create the ciphertext using the Vigenère table. Using the alphabet down the left side of the Vigenère table, find the row for the first letter of the keyword line. Since the first keyword letter is *A*, it will be the first row. Next, using the alphabet across the top of the Vigenère table, find the column for the first letter of the plaintext message. The first plaintext letter is *T*, so it is the column under that letter. Now find the letter where the row and the column intersect. The letter is *T*, so the first letter of the ciphertext is *T*.

Find the row for the second keyword letter, which is *L*. Find the column for the second plaintext letter, which is *H*. The letter at the intersection of this row and column is *S*, so *S* will be the second letter of the ciphertext.

Continue in the same way until the entire message is encrypted.

A B C D E F G H I J K L M N O P Q R S T U V W X Y Z

	A	B	C	D	E	F	G	H	I	J	K	L	M	N	O	P	Q	R	S	T	U	V	W	X	Y	Z
A	A	B	C	D	E	F	G	H	I	J	K	L	M	N	O	P	Q	R	S	T	U	V	W	X	Y	Z
B	B	C	D	E	F	G	H	I	J	K	L	M	N	O	P	Q	R	S	T	U	V	W	X	Y	Z	A
C	C	D	E	F	G	H	I	J	K	L	M	N	O	P	Q	R	S	T	U	V	W	X	Y	Z	A	B
D	D	E	F	G	H	I	J	K	L	M	N	O	P	Q	R	S	T	U	V	W	X	Y	Z	A	B	C
E	E	F	G	H	I	J	K	L	M	N	O	P	Q	R	S	T	U	V	W	X	Y	Z	A	B	C	D
F	F	G	H	I	J	K	L	M	N	O	P	Q	R	S	T	U	V	W	X	Y	Z	A	B	C	D	E
G	G	H	I	J	K	L	M	N	O	P	Q	R	S	T	U	V	W	X	Y	Z	A	B	C	D	E	F
H	H	I	J	K	L	M	N	O	P	Q	R	S	T	U	V	W	X	Y	Z	A	B	C	D	E	F	G
I	I	J	K	L	M	N	O	P	Q	R	S	T	U	V	W	X	Y	Z	A	B	C	D	E	F	G	H
J	J	K	L	M	N	O	P	Q	R	S	T	U	V	W	X	Y	Z	A	B	C	D	E	F	G	H	I
K	K	L	M	N	O	P	Q	R	S	T	U	V	W	X	Y	Z	A	B	C	D	E	F	G	H	I	J
L	L	M	N	O	P	Q	R	S	T	U	V	W	X	Y	Z	A	B	C	D	E	F	G	H	I	J	K
M	M	N	O	P	Q	R	S	T	U	V	W	X	Y	Z	A	B	C	D	E	F	G	H	I	J	K	L
N	N	O	P	Q	R	S	T	U	V	W	X	Y	Z	A	B	C	D	E	F	G	H	I	J	K	L	M
O	O	P	Q	R	S	T	U	V	W	X	Y	Z	A	B	C	D	E	F	G	H	I	J	K	L	M	N
P	P	Q	R	S	T	U	V	W	X	Y	Z	A	B	C	D	E	F	G	H	I	J	K	L	M	N	O
Q	Q	R	S	T	U	V	W	X	Y	Z	A	B	C	D	E	F	G	H	I	J	K	L	M	N	O	P
R	R	S	T	U	V	W	X	Y	Z	A	B	C	D	E	F	G	H	I	J	K	L	M	N	O	P	Q
S	S	T	U	V	W	X	Y	Z	A	B	C	D	E	F	G	H	I	J	K	L	M	N	O	P	Q	R
T	T	U	V	W	X	Y	Z	A	B	C	D	E	F	G	H	I	J	K	L	M	N	O	P	Q	R	S
U	U	V	W	X	Y	Z	A	B	C	D	E	F	G	H	I	J	K	L	M	N	O	P	Q	R	S	T
V	V	W	X	Y	Z	A	B	C	D	E	F	G	H	I	J	K	L	M	N	O	P	Q	R	S	T	U
W	W	X	Y	Z	A	B	C	D	E	F	G	H	I	J	K	L	M	N	O	P	Q	R	S	T	U	V
X	X	Y	Z	A	B	C	D	E	F	G	H	I	J	K	L	M	N	O	P	Q	R	S	T	U	V	W
Y	Y	Z	A	B	C	D	E	F	G	H	I	J	K	L	M	N	O	P	Q	R	S	T	U	V	W	X
Z	Z	A	B	C	D	E	F	G	H	I	J	K	L	M	N	O	P	Q	R	S	T	U	V	W	X	Y

Keyword: ALBER TIALB ERTIA LBERT IALBE RTIAL BERTI ALBER TIALB ERTIA
Plaintext: THEVI GENER ECIPH ERMAK ESCRY PTANA LYSIS MOREC HALLE NGING
Ciphertext: TSFZZ ZMNPS ITBXH PSQRD MSNSC GMINL MCJBA MZSIT AILWF RXBVG

You can see from this why frequency analysis isn't effective with a polyalphabetic substitution cipher. *E* is the most common letter in the plaintext; it occurs 8 times. However, this is masked by the fact that it is represented by 4 letters in the ciphertext: *F, M, P,* and *I*. On the other hand, *S* is the most common letter in the ciphertext, appearing 6 times, but it represents 3 different letters in the plaintext: *H, R,* and *S*.

For almost 300 years, the Vigenère cipher was considered unbreakable. Finally, in 1863, a method for breaking it was found. The method depends on finding the length of the keyword. The first step is to look for repeated bigrams, or pairs of letters, in the ciphertext. Repeated bigrams in the ciphertext aren't always the result of encryption of the same plaintext bigrams, but often they are. Repeated bigrams can provide the basis for breaking the Vigenère cipher.

If we check the ciphertext we just created, we find 3 repeated bigrams: *PS, SI,* and *IT*.

Keyword:	ALBER	TIALB	ERTIA	LBERT	IALBE	RTIAL	BERTI	ALBER	TIALB	ERTIA
Plaintext:	THEVI	GENER	ECIPH	ERMAK	ESCRY	PTANA	LYSIS	MOREC	HALLE	NGING
Ciphertext:	TSFZZ	ZMNPS	ITBXH	PSQRD	MSNSC	GMINL	MCJBA	MZSIT	AILWF	RXBVG

21

The next step is to count the letters between each bigram and its repetition. From the *P* in the first *PS* to the *P* in the second *PS*, we count 7 letters. The first *P* is the starting point, or 0, so the counting actually begins with the letter *S*, which is 1. From the *S* in the first *SI* to the *S* in the second *SI* is 28 letters. It's also 28 letters from the *I* in the first *IT* to the *I* in the second *IT*.

Now factor the distances between repeated bigrams to identify possible keyword lengths. The factors that occur most often are the most likely possibilities for the length of the keyword. Since 7 is a prime number, its factors are only 1 and 7. We can ignore 1, since a good keyword would have more than 1 letter. The factors for 28 are 1, 2, 4, 7, 14, and 28. Again, we can ignore 1. The only factor that occurs more than once for the numbers 7 and 28 is 7, making 7 the likely length of the keyword. Since for this example we actually know the keyword, we can check this prediction. The keyword is *ALBERTI*, which has 7 letters. You can see that this method works.

How does this help us? Remember that with the Vigenère cipher, each letter of the keyword tells us which row or alphabet of the Vigenère table is used to encrypt the corresponding letter of the plaintext. If the keyword is 7 letters, each seventh letter of the plaintext is encrypted using the same row or alphabet of the Vigenère table. Let's look again at our cryptogram.

Keyword: ALBER TIALB ERTIA LBERT IALBE RTIAL BERTI ALBER TIALB ERTIA

Ciphertext: TSFZZ ZMNPS ITBXH PSQRD MSNSC GMINL MCJBA MZSIT AILWF RXBVG

Now let's make a list of which letters of the ciphertext are encrypted with each letter of the keyword *(ALBERTI)*:

first keyword letter *(A)*:   T, N, H, S, N, M, L, G
second keyword letter *(L)*:   S, P, P, N, L, Z, W
third keyword letter *(B)*:   F, S, S, S, M, S, F
fourth keyword letter *(E)*:   Z, I, Q, C, C, I, R
fifth keyword letter *(R)*:   Z, T, R, G, J, T, X
sixth keyword letter *(T)*:   Z, B, D, M, B, A, B
seventh keyword letter *(I)*: M ,X, M, I, A, I, V

All the letters in each of the groups were encrypted using the same row or alphabet of the Vigenère table. Since each row is a Caesar cipher, we can apply frequency analysis to each group to crack the code for that group. Then we can put the decrypted letters together again in the correct order to read the message.

Cryptanalyzing a message written with the Vigenère cipher takes much longer than cryptanalyzing a message written with a Caesar cipher, but it can be done. If you found the process difficult to follow, don't feel bad. Remember, for almost 300 years, nobody thought the Vigenère cipher could be broken!

Transposition Ciphers

Both simple and polyalphabetic substitution ciphers involve replacing the letters in the plaintext to encrypt the message. With a **transposition** cipher, the letters in the plaintext aren't replaced, they're simply rearranged to form the ciphertext. Can this create secure secret messages? Let's look at a cryptogram written with a transposition cipher:

IEWTOPEATTTRHMSIPIEWNNNREEAOCGTRITTAWSCSSRHSHSSIAIE

It looks like a meaningless string of letters, doesn't it? Now let's look at the plaintext from which the cryptogram was created:

THIS SECRET MESSAGE WAS WRITTEN WITH A TRANSPOSITION CIPHER.

How was this plaintext transformed into the cryptogram? It was done using the best-known method of transposition, simple **columnar** transposition. Let's go through the process step-by-step to see how it works.

The first step is choosing a keyword. The keyword chosen for this example was *REARRANGE*. Next, a number is assigned to each letter in the keyword following alphabetical order. If the same letter appears more than once, numbers are assigned according to the order of appearance in the word. Following the alphabet, first *A* in *REARRANGE* is 1. Since *A* appears twice, the second *A* is 2. *E* is the next letter of the alphabet to appear in *REARRANGE*, and *E* appears twice. The first *E* becomes 3, and the second *E* becomes 4. Numbering continues in this way until each letter in *REARRANGE* has a number.

R	E	A	R	R	A	N	G	E
7	3	1	8	9	2	6	5	4

Ancient Greek warriors from Sparta, like those shown in this carving from 525 B.C., are said to have used a transposition cipher to send secret messages. A strip of leather was wrapped around a cylinder and a message written on it. When the strip was unwound, it had only a random collection of letters. The message could only be read by wrapping the strip around another cylinder with the same diameter as the original cylinder.

Next, write the plaintext message from page 24 in rows under the keyword, as shown below. Leave no spaces between the words in the message.

R	E	A	R	R	A	N	G	E
7	3	1	8	9	2	6	5	4
T	H	I	S	S	E	C	R	E
T	M	E	S	S	A	G	E	W
A	S	W	R	I	T	T	E	N
W	I	T	H	A	T	R	A	N
S	P	O	S	I	T	I	O	N
C	I	P	H	E	R			

To create the ciphertext, start by writing the letters from the column with the number 1: IEWTOP. Follow this with the letters from column 2, then the letters from column 3, and so on. Leave no spaces between the groups of letters. This produces the cryptogram we saw at the beginning of this chapter:

IEWTOPEATTTRHMSIPIEWNNNREEAOCGTRITTAWSCSSRHSHSSIAIE

A person who received a cryptogram written with a simple columnar transposition cipher would need to know the keyword in order to decrypt the message.

Another type of transposition cipher is the rail fence cipher. In the rail fence cipher, the message is written in rows that resemble the rails of a fence. This is what gives the cipher its name. Let's go through the steps of encrypting a message using the rail fence cipher.

Different numbers of rails can be used in the rail fence cipher. We'll choose to use 3 rails. Here's the message we want to encrypt:

TRANSPOSITION CIPHERS ARE VERY ANCIENT.

The message is encrypted by starting on the top "rail" and writing downward, 1 letter per rail. After reaching the bottom "rail," the next letter goes on the top rail, and the sequence starts again.

T	N	O	T	N	P	R	R	E	A	I	T
R	S	S	I	C	H	S	E	R	N	E	X
A	P	I	O	I	E	A	V	Y	C	N	Z

You'll notice that there are 2 extra letters at the end of the message: X and Z. These are called nulls. They are added to make sure each row has the same number of letters and to confuse anyone trying to break the cipher.

The next step in the encryption is to write out the arrangement of letters as they appear on the "rails," without any breaks. The top rail comes first, then the middle rail, then the bottom rail.

TNOTNPRREAITRSSICHSERNEXAPIOIEAVYCNZ

The final cryptogram is created by dividing the long string of letters into words of fixed length, usually 5 letters.

TNOTN PRREA ITRSS ICHSE RNEXA PIOIE AVYCN Z

Now let's try cryptanalyzing a ciphertext created using the rail fence cipher. Cryptanalyzing a message written with the rail fence cipher requires that we know the number of rails, so let's say our ciphertext was written with 3 rails. Here's the message:

MYOEN RTAST EERNO YAPPF DYALI OAWDG BQNEL ICPNY SBRAI HBX

The first step is to get rid of the spaces so there is 1 long string of letters.

MYOENRTASTEERNOYAPPFDYALIOAWDGBQNELICPNYSBRAIHBX

Now, we know that there are an equal number of letters in each rail of a message written with the rail fence cipher, so count the number of letters, then divide by 3—the number of rails—and arrange the letters into 3 equal groups. In this case, each group has 16 letters.

MYOENRTASTEERNOY | APPFDYALIOAWDGBQ | NELICPNYSBRAIHBX

Arrange the groups into rails. The first group will be the top rail, the second group will be the middle rail, and the third group will be the bottom rail.

M	Y	O	E	N	R	T	A	S	T	E	E	R	N	O	Y
A	P	P	F	D	Y	A	L	I	O	A	W	D	G	B	Q
N	E	L	I	C	P	N	Y	S	B	R	A	I	H	B	X

Next, write down the letters starting with the *M* on the top rail, followed by the *A* on the middle rail and the *N* on the bottom rail. Return to the top rail for the next letter, and continue in this fashion.

MANYPEOPLEFINDCRYPTANALYSISTOBEAREWARDINGHOBBYQX

Finally, break the string of letters into easily identifiable words.

MANY PEOPLE FIND CRYPTANALYSIS TO BE A REWARDING HOBBY QX

The *Q* and *X* at the end are nulls. Get rid of them, and you have the message!

In 1586, a plot to kill Queen Elizabeth I was discussed in an encrypted letter. The plot was discovered when agents for Elizabeth I captured the letter and cryptanalyzed it.

29

The ciphers in this book are all known as pencil-and-paper systems because encryption and decryption can be done using only a pencil and paper. They are just a few of the many ciphers developed over the centuries. Some ciphers required machines, such as the famous **Enigma** Machine used by the German army in World War II. Both pencil-and-paper and machine ciphers were commonly used to send messages containing military and political secrets. In our modern information age, the best-known uses of cryptography are quite different.

Today, cryptography is used to make sure that information stored electronically is secure. It is also used to secure information sent over the Internet. When you purchase something over the Internet, you may transmit credit card information. That information is encrypted to protect it from thieves. The encryption method is far more complicated than any of the ciphers we've examined. Complex mathematical **algorithms** accomplish the encryption. Since thieves are always trying to break the codes, cryptographers are always working on new algorithms. Like all cryptographers before them, they hope to create a code that can't be broken. Who knows—if you keep developing your math skills, perhaps one day you'll be the cryptographer who invents the unbreakable cipher!

Glossary

algorithm (AL-guh-rih-thum) A step-by-step system for solving a mathematical problem.

cipher (SY-fuhr) A method of transforming a text to conceal its meaning.

columnar (kuh-LUHM-nuhr) Relating to or characterized by columns.

cryptanalyze (krip-TA-nuh-lyz) To solve a cryptogram.

cryptogram (KRIP-tuh-gram) A message written with a cipher.

cryptographer (krip-TAH-gruh-fuhr) A specialist in cryptography.

cryptography (krip-TAH-gruh-fee) The encrypting and decrypting of messages written with a cipher.

decrypt (dee-KRIPT) To decode something written with a cipher.

encrypt (ihn-KRIPT) To write something in code using a cipher.

enigma (ih-NIHG-muh) An obscure speech or writing.

Hebrew (HEE-broo) A member of or descendant from an ancient group of people who spoke the Hebrew language.

keyword (KEE-wuhrd) A word that is necessary to decrypt a message written with a cipher.

polyalphabetic (pah-lee-al-fuh-BEH-tihk) Having several alphabets.

reciprocal (rih-SIH-pruh-kuhl) Mutually corresponding.

transposition (trans-puh-ZIH-shun) The act or process of rearranging.

Index